ONE BY TWO

Oninthough

Chennai • Bangalore

CLEVER FOX PUBLISHING
Chennai, India

Published by CLEVER FOX PUBLISHING 2024
Copyright © Oninthough 2024

All Rights Reserved.
ISBN: 978-93-56489-52-3

This book has been published with all reasonable efforts taken to make the material error-free after the consent of the author. No part of this book shall be used, reproduced in any manner whatsoever without written permission from the author, except in the case of brief quotations embodied in critical articles and reviews.

The Author of this book is solely responsible and liable for its content including but not limited to the views, representations, descriptions, statements, information, opinions and references ["Content"]. The Content of this book shall not constitute or be construed or deemed to reflect the opinion or expression of the Publisher or Editor. Neither the Publisher nor Editor endorse or approve the Content of this book or guarantee the reliability, accuracy or completeness of the Content published herein and do not make any representations or warranties of any kind, express or implied, including but not limited to the implied warranties of merchantability, fitness for a particular purpose. The Publisher and Editor shall not be liable whatsoever for any errors, omissions, whether such errors or omissions result from negligence, accident, or any other cause or claims for loss or damages of any kind, including without limitation, indirect or consequential loss or damage arising out of use, inability to use, or about the reliability, accuracy or sufficiency of the information contained in this book.

About the Author

Oninthough is an award-winning stand-up comedian, author & poet, and artist.

He is amongst the select few multilingual (trilingual) poets in India. He has written 500+ poems across three languages (English, Hindi, and Bengali), a novel, and more than a dozen short stories. His works have been featured by the reputed English daily, The Statesman. He was awarded an Honourable Mention at India's Next Big Writer, 2021. His debut novel "Ticking Thirty – Delayed Identity Crisis or Premature Midlife Crisis?" won the Authors Gully Book Writing Competition, and was published on April 1st, 2022. He also won the Ukiyoto Literary Award: Top 30 Books (Fiction) To Look Out For In 2022, and the Cinemura Award: Top 20 Books To Look Out For Film Adaptation in 2022, besides winning the Fireboxx Best Debut Author Award and the Fireboxx Best Fiction Book Award for the novel. Oninthough is also a recipient of the 21st Century Emily Dickinson Award, for poetry. His second book was an anthology of poems, titled, "Midnight Musings Of A Madman", that was published on February 10, 2023. He was also an Official Shortlist for the Wingword Poetry Prize, 2023.

As a stand-up comedian, he has performed for audiences across 20+ cities, 7 nations, and 3 continents. His stand-up comedy content has more than 3 million views across social media.

Oninthough has often been featured for his monochrome art, especially portraits and stippling art, niches he's carved quite the name for himself, in.

About the Book

One By Two is a carefully curated collection of poems, half of them in English, the other half, in Hindi.

One By Two is Oninthough's second anthology of poems to be published, following **Midnight Musings Of A Madman**, published in 2023, and his first body of bilingual work.

One By Two brings together forty-eight of Oninthough's selected poetic works, penned between 2017 and 2023.

Acknowledgement

I would like to acknowledge the extraordinary debt I owe to the genes passed on to me, from the paternal side of affairs, given, it comes off two generations and half a dozen books of poetry. There are two things that have been predominantly passed on from one generation to another, for the third generation in a row: migraine & poetry. Whether there was an option to choose just the latter, one would never know!

I also owe this to that classmate of mine, back in third grade, who challenged me to write rhymes, because that's really where my journey with words for poesy, began!

Contents

All Of What I Have - (10)
औकात - (11)
The Beginning Of The End - (13)
इंसान भी आख़िर सुट्टा ही है - (14)
Your Beard Smells Of Old Smoke - (15)
एक और कहानी - (17)
What's In A Name - (18)
मरीज़-ए-मोहब्बत - (19)
Where'd The Stories Go - (20)
अर्ज़ियाँ - (21)
The Goodnight Lullaby - (22)
ग़ज़ल-ए-मौत - (25)
The Last Love Letter - (26)
नकाब - (27)
Hail The Insane - (28)
शायरी ज़िन्दगी की - (30)
The Flight Of A Falcon - (31)
टाइम टाइम की बात है - (42)
The Ballad Of A Lamenting Lunatic - (43)
मुझे दो पल सांस लेना है - (48)

I'd Roll A Joint - (49)
रूह - (50)
Pulp Fiction - (51)
खोटा सिक्का - (52)
Not Your Chaste Woman - (53)
हम सब नशे में है - (55)
Pisces - (56)
सारांश - (57)
The Rebel From A Revolution - (58)
लैला मजनू - (65)
Lambrequin - (66)
बेघर रिश्ते - (67)
Collateral Friction - (68)
काश - (69)
The Skin Of Your Love - (70)
बिकाऊ - (73)
An Unlikely Homecoming - (74)
सब ठीक हो जाएगा - (75)
Frozen In Forever - (76)
बस घर रह जाते है - (77)
Bad Blood - (78)
रंग बेरंग - (80)
What Is It Like - (81)
इतिहास-शास्त्र - (84)

Have You Loved Enough - (85)
इंसान मादरचोद है - (86)
I'm Scared Of Days But I'm Scared Of Nights More - (87)
अंत से शुरू - (89)

All Of What I Have

I have scars from the times I healed, and, tattoos from the times I couldn't

I have stories from the times I could re-live all over again, and, poetry from the times I didn't want to live even once

I have laughs from the times I pulled through and an ego to clothe them in, and, I have tears from the times I just couldn't, and many a mouthful of whiskey to drown them in

I have an insatiable urge to live for what the times to come might be, and, an irresistible urge to die for what the times to come will never be

औकात

ये जो औकात की बात है आप करते रहते हो
कहां बिकती है ये औकात?

आप के महलों में जो ख़्वाब महकती है
उसी ख्वाब के कई भूले बिसरे पन्ने
हम भी पलटते हैं अपनी सस्ती दीवारों पर बराबर
आप के शहरों में जो जिंदगी बस्ती है
उसकी जिंदगी के कुछ घिसी-पीटी लम्हे
हम भी पलटते हैं अपने कांच की चूड़ियों में
आप के रंगीन शरबतों में जो नशा चढ़ता है

हमारी भीगी आंखें भी धुत्त हो जाती है उसके नशे में
क्योंकि हमारी वो औकात कहां के हम आप जैसे बने?

आप की हकीकत हमारा गुरुर बैन
जाता है
आप की साँसें हमारा क़त्ल-ए-आम

ये जो औकात की बात है आप करते रहते
हो कितने की कीमत में बिकती है ये
औकात?

The Beginning Of The End

If death wasn't an obvious
Would life still be as precious?
If endings weren't an obvious

Would beginnings still be as ambitious?

इंसान भी आख़िर सुट्टा ही है

इंसान भी आख़िर सुट्टा ही है

दो पाल की कागज़ात मौजुदगी
बस जल के राख होने की राह देख रही है
जिंदगी तो बस माचिस की तीली है
इंसान भी आख़िर सुट्टा ही है

Your Beard Smells Of Old Smoke

"Your beard smells of old smoke", you'd once said.

I wish I could have told you of all the times, every time I rewound the poetry in the skin of a singular sentence
I wish I could have told you, how your hair smells of night jasmine; how a man of orchids had given in to the essence of a night jasmine's flourish
I wish I could have told you of the monochrome desires bleeding in the heart of the neon citylights and pastel lives; pastels have always been exaggerated, monochromes misunderstood

Beyond glass existences and pretended conversations, lies an entirety of restless unsettling essays; unpenned scribbles that made nightmares look lullabies
Beyond plastic flesh and ceramic bones, lies the whole of faceless demons and nameless fears; skeletons lurk in dark, blank spaces

In a war of similars and congruents, differences drew first blood
Between candids and corpses, second chances hung from semicolons

I could have resurrected and called it Renaissance
I could have scripted good mornings in goodnight kisses

But, this time, I'll let it all out, at a full stop
I am tired of beginnings that end

एक और कहानी

एक कवि
करो दोस्त
तीसरी मंजिल

हज़ारों बिखरे ख्वाहिशें
आख़िर में बस एक और कहानी है
एक और कहानी खबरों की सुरखियाँ में
एक और कहानी क़ब्रों की भूले बिसरे

पन्नो में

What's In A Name

Where had she come from
Where was she leaving to

What did she call herself in the silences
Who was she beyond and beneath her

I knew nothing; none of it at all

And yet, the eyes met
No comets fell
No meteors rose
And yet, the rains lashed the feeble city lives
And yet, the silences thundered the voices in the head
Not a moment stood still
Not a word was spilled

And yet, there was poetry in the blood and in the bones
And yet, there was life and there was death, wrapped in the skin

मरीज-ए-मोहब्बत

खुदा तो बस एक मोहरा है
जिन्हे ज़माने ने बदनाम किया

प्यार तो बस एक मुशायरा है
जिन्हे मतलबियों ने मोहब्बत का नाम दिया

Where'd The Stories Go

Where do you think the stories go, at the end of it all

Dawns always make good mornings
Dusks often are buried alive in obituaries

But then, what happens to the stories when the lives in them leave them for dead

Are they buried, burnt, or, just sprinkled in the blank spaces, between pretended existences
Who tells the tales of the stories

अर्जियाँ

अर्जियाँ
कुछ तुम्हारे
कुछ मात्र

और बाकी जो रह गये
वो गुमनाम हुए

अर्जियाँ में

The Goodnight Lullaby

The length of an entirety, the entirety you call home, wrapped in four fragile failing walls
And yet, I can feel myself choking on the dead air, as if sinking to the very entrails of a filthy ocean
The whole of a crowd, thick and filling, somewhat like a never-ending horde of blood-thirsty locusts
And yet, I can feel myself strangulated, my windpipe left for dead, in a loveless foreplay, with the comfortably unsettling silences of a ransacked cemetery

I still remember the night

It was a usual night with an unusual sky, patches of pale crimson and a tinge of beige smothered right across the ribs
It was the night I had freed my wife
I had freed my wife from the woman living in her bones
For, my wife was in love with me while the woman inside had rented out her flesh
And I couldn't watch her tear apart my love, gradually, inches by the skin
So, I held the woman, firm by the throat
And dug my fingers in
Fingers don't cut through; fingers dig deep and blunt
She blushed as if shot in blood as I felt her neck break and wilt like a spineless invertebrate nightcrawler
And then, I cut her equal, right between the breasts, all the way down, till the very end
The woman bled as my wife watched it all, in assuring stoic silence
But, the woman still had my wife's face on her

And, I had to conclude what I had begun
So I sat down to work, yet again
And as I carved her out and chiselled
through the thinning lumps of flesh
I watched my wife's face disappear, bit
by bit, somewhat like the setting sun
across the fading horizon

My wife. My mother. My father.
I freed them all
One by one, one at a time

The idea of singulars is beautiful

But, what do I do of these lives
A pistol to his head, a bullet in mine
A knife to her mouth, a blade in mine
How do I free them all

Too many dead to be put to rest
Too few hour hands on the wall clock to
cleanse them all

Tonight, let me lose another night's sleep as I put to sleep another goodnight

ग़ज़ल-ए-मौत

तू मोहब्बत थी मेरी या ज़रूरी

मोहब्बत मरीज़ बनती है
ज़रुरतें बेबस
कभी आदतों में प्यार ढूंढ कर देख

मोहब्बत में शायर और ज़रुरत में
लाचार तो बने बहुत शहीद
कभी खुद से प्यार करके देख

मौत भी ग़ज़ल बन जायेगी

The Last Love Letter

Have you ever looked up the midnight sky wondering if the star-crossed love ballads have made their way beyond the cursed clouds?
Have you ever lost your very existence in the midst of a nowhere cramped up for blanks, pondering over the scent of possibilities in a singular fragrance?

Have you ever woken off a tender slumber, fingers losing their way in the abyss beneath the thighs, the canopy of hair eclipsing the contoured terrains across the ribs, minutes away from what remained of the umbilicus, mauling the very idea of outlines as you breathed my poetry in your skin?

If you have, you'd know where to find me.

नक़ाब

कांच के पुतलों में
कभी आसमान का नक़ाब देखे हो

थोड़ा सा नीला बांट सा सफेद
उस नक़ाब के पीछे दबे हज़ारों ज़िंदगियां
मेरी कहानी कहीं बंध पड़ी है
एक अजीब सी घुटन जैसी

क्या तुम उन्हें मुझे लौटा सकते हो

Hail The Insane

What do you call them
Legends in love
Or
Martyrs from a Micawberish matinee

What did they get right
Where might have you gone wrong
You have often wondered
Haven't you

No
Nothing right
Nothing wrong

Magnum opuses don't come with a recipe

It's the arrogance to stay insane
It's the disdain to become maverick madmen in an obsessed world waging wars for the sake of sanity in the name of equality

Sane is a dystopian folklore; hail the insane

शायरी जिन्दगी की

जाने की ज़िद भी एक ख़्वाब ही है
आने जाने के बीच में कलाम लीए
जिंदगी एक शायर ही तो है

पता बदल जाता है
आदतें नये चश्में ढूंढते है

घूम हुए सवालों का जवाब भी
आख़िर शायरी हाय तो है

The Flight Of A Falcon

Once upon a time
A long time ago
There lived a falcon.

A meaty coat of monochromed feathers
Piercing eyes, somewhat like the colorless toy marbles of a childhood
A peach dark nebula at the very nucleus of it
A pair of wings, far-flung and overarching

He would wake every morning to the daybreak atop the towering arm of a faraway eucalyptus

The entirety still like the stagnant tranquil of the seas before the storm
The eyes, restless like the flight of a newborn.

It was an everyday
The sun was setting to the southern winds across the western skies
The falcon was homeward bound
It was supper time

As he sailed through the skies one last time
Something crossed his eyes
Something at the very heart of the unkempt jungles
Something miles away, a distant blur that could be forgotten in the open eyes

But, the falcon was too exact to miss out on specifics.

And so, he aimed and he aimed well
He cut right through the throat of the jungle

If only he knew, that moment onward, everything would just pave the road to a revolution
A revolution like no other
A revolution like no other apparently

It was a cassowary.

The thorns of a shrub had cut her
There was blood, and a lot more pain
But, the cassowary was too disdained to plead for help; if only narcissism had a cure

The falcon stayed the night
The night after
And, the nights after

Twelve nights after, she had healed
But, the falcon couldn't leave
Neither did the cassowary ask him to

What heals us is often what breaks us.

As the day broke, the falcon stood next to the cassowary, his right wing spread across her
The flight of love, they'd call it.

"But I can't fly", the cassowary cried
"I will fly for us", the falcon smiled
"And I'll build ground", she smiled

"But, what about a home?", she was pensive

"Home is here", the falcon smiled in an unusual calm

It was an improbable wedding
But, a wedding nevertheless.

It was all good
The falcon fetched
The cassowary gathered
It was family

And then, one morning, parenthood embraced them
Four fledglings
The falcon kissed the cassowary to the meek shrills of the newborns

As the sun went past the mahogany and the fish
And the moon shone with all her grace in the mid-sky

The cassowary lay awake
She was tired, she was sleepy, but yet, wide awake

"What's bothering you?", the falcon asked
"What if they can't fly?", the cassowary was disturbed
"They don't need to know they were born to fly", the falcon smiled
"But, what do we tell them?", the cassowary asked
"Nothing. They are what we are. And, we don't fly", the falcon said
"But you do fly!" she exclaimed
"Not anymore" he smiled

The falcon went fetching the next morning
Only that, this time, the skies were different

The time was lost in the tides

The high and the low

The fledglings had grown up
The skies were nothing but the skies to them
They called the jungle their home

They were what they were told they were.
Aren't we all?

And one day, they found love too.

The family wasn't about just a family anymore.

The falcon was gone.
The cassowary was gone.

But, what nobody knew was, with them was gone the truth of a hundred thousand lives

What lived on wasn't a lie
What isn't a lie is not the truth either

The half-truth of a lifetime had become the folklore of the ages.

The folklore we all wish we could afford to not believe
The folklore we all think we could believe was just another tale
The folklore we all desire to re-write someday

But then, what more are desires than mere desires?

Every revolution begins with an absurd idea of a madman.

How could this be any different?

One day, a madman wanted to rewrite the folklore
For the first time in years, someone was willing to risk it all

But, so much for re-writing a folklore?
If only someone could convince the madman to otherwise.

He was laughed at
He was scorned at
He was cursed at
He was lamented at

But then, a madman is a madman.

And so, he spread his wings and leaped
He fell straight on his face
The jungle called it "the fall of a lunatic"

Death haven't deterred madmen

This was just a fall.

He tried one more time
He fell one more time
He tried one more time and one more
He fell again. Again. Again.

Broken bones. Bruised eyes. A bleeding beak.
The madman took one last leap
This fall would kill him

And, as the jungle let out a sigh in an anticipation of the inevitable
The madman flew.

The wind was too strong
The wings were too weak
The entirety of his strengths and beliefs could suffice for just a flight

The madman had his last fall
The jungle called it "the flight of freedom"

The madman had just begun a revolution
The equations had changed
The roadside lunatic of a yesterday was the legend of today

If only the world could afford legends while they were still alive

Today, everyone wants to fly
Today, no one wants to call the jungles their home
Today, everyone is aiming for the skies

Some fly
Some few die trying

The others just sit there, watching the flight of a falcon, and complaining of prejudice.

टाइम टाइम की बात है

टाइम टाइम की बात है

कभी लकीरें खिंच जाती हैं, कभी माँगें
कभी शहद बरस जाते हैं, कभी बारिशें

कभी होठों की बातें जुबां बराबर खड़े कफन बंधे
कभी आँखों की नमी काजल की लहरों में बेशरम

सब टाइम टाइम की बात है

The Ballad Of A Lamenting Lunatic

I couldn't be the son you wanted
But trust me, I tried
I couldn't be the friend you wanted
But trust me, I tried
I couldn't be the brother you wanted
But trust me, I tried
I couldn't be the lover you wanted
But trust me, I tried

I tried it all
I tried not being the mess you see around

I tried not being the disaster you think I am
I tried it all

But, aren't we all entitled to failures?

I could never become the son you would have wanted me to
I could never let you in those dark alleys I sleep to every night
I could never live all of that dreamy life you had promised yourself to let me have
I could never do any of it

Did I want to?

Maybe I did, but maybe, just maybe, I wanted a life I could call my own more than a life of unnecessary debts and continual regrets

Is it too audacious to live for yourself for once?

I could never become the friend you would have wanted me to
I could never let you in all of my uncomfortable that I house
I could never be the midnight kerchief to your torments and tears
I could never do any of it

Did I want to?

Maybe I did, but maybe, just maybe, I had too many demons taking shape in the entrails, demons I couldn't let loose

Is it too harsh to live for yourself for once?

I could never become the brother you would have wanted me to

I could never let you in the open scars I hide behind the hundred smiles
I could never be the cornerstone you could look up to in your times of distraught
I could never do any of it

Did I want to?
Maybe I did, but maybe, just maybe, I had too many stories of my own, too many loose ends that could never be mended

Is it too ruthless to live for yourself for once?

I could never become the lover you would have wanted me to
I could never let you in the thousand tales that keep me awake every single night

I could never be the eyes every time you wanted to see the world just a bit differently
I could never do any of it

Did I want to?

Maybe I did, but maybe, just maybe, I was too scared to let you bleed every time you trod on the broken pieces of me like they were your morning meadow

Is it too dead to live for yourself for once?

Maybe I could have saved you all.

But then, who'd save me?

मुझे दो पल सांस लेना है

रूठे को मनाया जा सकता है
बीते को भुलाया जा सकता है

जो धूल बन के बिखर गए
उन्हें आसमानों में पनाह मिल गया
जो बारूद की महक में पता ढूँढ़ने चले थे
आग की दरिया में उनको घर मिल गई

पर जिन्हे जल्दी थी
घर लौटने की
ट्रेन छूट जाने की
वो रुके नहीं

उन्हें रोकना बेवज़ह है जिनकी सांसें मैं रेल की पटरी बिछी हो
टूटे जिंदगी और बिछड़े सपनों की दौड़ में मुझे दो पल सांस लेना है

I'd Roll A Joint

The paper lies they feed us in the name of history

The fallen governments they sell us in the name of democracy

The absurd wars they make believe us in the name of equality

If I could burn them all

I'd roll a joint

रूह

पल भर में मौसम बदल गया था
गुमनाम सांसों को ठिकाना मिल गई थी

हाथों में मेहंदी के लिए किसी और का
नाम के कदम तले तुम चले थे मोहब्बत
फ़रमाने

रूह की रुख मोड़ पाए फिर?

Pulp Fiction

Imagine.

Imagine a reality
A reality untouched by the truth
A world of stories

Stories; heart-wrenching,
adrenaline-rushing, spine-chilling,
tear-jerking
Stories; realities and parallel realities of
a pulp fiction

Stories inspired by actualities; stories nevertheless
Stories for company in the early morning commode
Stories they sell in the name of journalism
Stories I flush down the stinky toilet highway

खोटा सिक्का

दुनिया तेज़ भाग रही है

जिंदगी ने भी रफ़्तार पकड़ ली

बस रिश्तों की अहमियत गिरती रहती है

जैसे गिरते रहते हैं पैसे की कीमत

हम तुम सब बस खोटे सिक्के बन के रह गये

Not Your Chaste Woman

I'm not your chaste woman.

No
I am not.

The woman you thought you had made a lesser mortal of
The woman you wanted to assault in the wrinkles of your stinking bed sheets
The woman you desired every morning every night and in the betweens

The woman you wished could be all about you and just you
The woman you felt you could cripple with the bruises and swollen wombs
The woman you had imagined you could tame in the lashes of your fallen chivalry

I'm none of it.
I'm not
Not any of it.

I am the woman who seeks for her lurching appetites
I am the woman who is beyond the idea of your holy grail of virginity
I am the woman who chooses her choices and her consequences
I am the woman who is complete in her world of sense and insane

I'm the woman.

This woman.
All of it.

I am no hero
I am no angel
I am no messiah
I am just a woman, any woman and every woman
I am just a woman; just not your chaste woman

हम सब नशे में हैं

नशे में हम सब हैं

कोई झूठ में धुत, कहानियों की आड़ में
कोई शराब की आगोश में, जिंदगी का बहाना दे कर

Pisces

Why this unrelenting pretense
As if we could ever really know the other

When have we really known each other

We are all strangers
A little less
A little more
Fishes losing shore in the ellipse of a glass bowl

Let's not know each other
Let's not understand what lies within and what lies beyond
Let the strangeness grow familiar instead
Almost like a habit
The stranger fishes knocking on the walls
Sinking in the surreal familiarity of stranger worlds

Until one day the walls break
And
All the worlds they knew perish

Have you seen a fish swim ashore when the seas have dried

<u>सारांश</u>

टूट के बिखर मत जाना

कांच के टुकड़ों में बस कुछ ज़ख्म होते हैं

जल के समा जाना

राख की बारिश में आसमान भी धुंधला पढ़ जाता है

The Rebel From A Revolution

Rebel isn't an idea
Rebel isn't a perspective
Rebel isn't an abstract
Rebel is just an epithet

One more of those hundred names you call out everyday defining all of what couldn't be outlined in your thesaurus of explanations

Revolution though is an idea

An idea that cherishes hope
A hope that serves life

Revolution isn't about rebels coming of age
Revolution isn't about the legends who script sagas

Revolution is you
Revolution is me
Revolution is us
All of us
Each and every in the singulars and the plurals
Every crumb of what we are
Every dime of who we are
Every grain of what we would not
Every slice of who we could not

In awareness and in intuit
We feed a revolution everyday
We breathe a revolution every ticking hour hand of the racing wall clock

Does that make us revolutionaries

We are no revolutionary
We are the revolution

And yet we cast away existences in the name of rebel
Call them outliers
Burn them in the name of democracy
Until we become them

We are all rebels
For
We all do have questions

Questions for the God
Questions for the Government
Questions for the definitions

Questions for the sanity
Questions for the answers we are told to be answers

And yet just some of us turn rebels
And the rest of us call them names condemning them in the name of oddity

Where did it all go wrong
Where did the equations fall apart
Where did the symphonies lose their rhythm
Where did the men and the women forget their voices

Too many have given up on the idea of questions
For questions turn you anarchists
For questions make you anti-nationals
For questions burn down houses
For questions bleed in bullet wounds

For questions scathe the very being of us

For questions aren't mere questions; questions are death notes for the cowards we have made of us
The cowards inhabit the world
Every one life till the very last of them
They are all cowards
We are all cowards

It's all a tale of cowards and lesser cowards

There are
Cowards who look death in the eye
Cowards who shiver down their broken spines
Cowards who are trapped in the making of history
Cowards who turn corpses in search of revolution

And then
There are
Cowards who seek comfort in the denial of realities
Cowards spineless crawling up the ribs of spined carcasses
Cowards who script history to suit their purposes
Cowards who die in their breath everyday
What do cowards know of revolution

But the revolution is here
And it will burn us all

What is revolution without a few spent lives
What is revolution without a few costed deaths

लैला मजनू

क़ुर्बान मजनू में लैला की आशिक़ी
आख़िर निस्वार्थ था या था बस चूतिया
कभी सोचे हो, पूछे हो अपने आप से
नहीं, क्यों जमाना कहा वो आशिक था

इश्क़ में क़ब्र खुद जाए तो आशिक़ी
और जिंदा लाश बन जाए तो बर्बादी

पर, किसने तय किया ये? और कैसे?

Lambrequin

When the walls
Of
A home
Your home

Weep in the odd blotches
Crack open right below the wrinkles
Bare the scars in the skin of cobwebs

What do you do

Rescue
Or
Wreck

Walls

Just four walls

Could they suffice
To
House a home
Your home

बेघर रिश्तें

जो रिश्ते खून से हो

कई बार खून में ही धुल जाते हैं

रिश्तों को घर देने के लिए बनी ऊंची मकानों में

कई बार रिश्तें ही बेघर रह जाते हैं

Collateral Friction

Aren't we all
Fluttering butterflies
In our world of rainbow puddles and
bewildered manholes

Aren't we all
Trembling fledglings
In our cosmos of crawling walls and
comfortable silences

Aren't we all
All of what we wouldn't ever be
otherwise

Reality is a parallel perspective

काश

काश..

दीवारों में दरारों की तरह रिश्तों
में दरारे के लिए भी सीमेंट ही काफी है होता

काश..

टूटी कांच पे चलने से मिले घाव की

तरह टूटे रिश्तों पे फ़िसलने से मिले
ज़ख्मों को भी मरहम ही काफी होता

The Skin Of Love

You say you love me

You say you love me
With every inch of your bare skin
You say you love me
With the entirety of your essence
You say you love me
With the whole of your being

And I believe you

But

What about the man you loved last
What about the man you loved before the last
What about the man you loved before him
What about all the men you loved

Didn't you love them all

With the whole of you
And yet
Every time another love story died
You wept at the funeral
And as time would have it
You put together every broken piece back together
And there you stood
As whole as ever

Can cello-tapes heal broken mirrors

What are we but remnants
From the last broken pieces
What are we but skeletons
Seeking hidden corners of living closets
What are we but ghosts
Sleeping to the ghouls of a recent bygone

Love fits right in paperback
The skin knows nothing but the skin

बिकाऊ

ज़बानी तो खरीद के लिए
ज़ुबान कैसे खरीदोगे

ख़बरें तो बाज़ारों में बिकती हैं
पर रीढ़ की हड्डी कैसे खरीदोगे

An Unlikely Homecoming

The untamed fragrance of the wildlings
had invaded the streets
One last time
Bridges crumbled and walls burnt at the
distance of radio sets and telephones
One more time

It was the season of the demon's fall
She had arrived

Happiness sprinkled across the skin in
goosebumps

सब ठीक हो जाएगा

सब ठीक नहीं होगा
कुछ भी ठीक नहीं होगा
बस अलग अलग हिसो में बँट कर टूटते रहोगे
और फिर एक दिन वो ही अलग अलग है
एक आग में जल के राख बना कर बिखर जाएगा
मिट्टी में मिल जाएगा रेत बन कर

सब ठीक हो जाएगा

बस पन्नो में लिखा एक और चूतिया का ख्वाब बन के रह जाएगा

Frozen In Forever

Seconds
Minutes
Hours
Days
Weeks
Months
Years

We keep striking moments
One after another
Off assigned shares of a lifetime

We are rushing to death in weighed forevers

बस घाव रह जाते हैं

कुछ नुकसान कभी नहीं होता
समय के साथ सूख जाता है बस
जिंदगी खर्च हो जाती है
सूखे पत्ते बेह जाते हैं पहली बारिश में

बस घाव रह जाते हैं

Bad Blood

    Tonight

I cut myself open
A cut here
A cut there
A cut over another and yet another

    Until

The walls smell of fresh flesh
The fresh scars lose clarity
The flesh stops longing for flesh

Blood

On the walls
On the patterned mosaic
On the sheets
On the blunt edges of the rusted knife
On the blood
On the horizons of the bare skin

Tonight

I cut myself open
A cut here
A cut there
A cut over another and yet another

Until

The skin doesn't smell of you anymore

The blood doesn't feel like you anymore
The very last drop of me isn't you anymore

Bad blood

रंग बेरंग

अजीब दास्तान है
रंग लगाने को त्योहार कहते हैं

रंग बदलने को जिंदगी

What Is It Like

What is it like inside that head of yours

The glass palaces you built of the mud castles
What is it like when it's all gone with the west wind, in the hungry tides

The wasted mongrel by the street you believed to be your cursed prince
What is it like when a hundred kisses later the mongrel still barks, the dreams

slipping right through the crevices of
your trembling fingers

The inexpensive love ballads you fancied
to be hymns penned for you
What is it like when the words are lost in
the startling truths of stenched corpses
and sinking worlds

What is it like when the rhapsody wears
off
What is it like when you wake off the
slumber

इतिहास-शास्त्र

कहने वाले कहते हैं

सेकड़ो साल पहले एक बंदा
शुद्धता का सबूत मांग के बीवी जलया था

उसे भगवान मान ने वाले का प्रयोग करें

देश की शुद्धि मांग के

उसी आग में आज देश जल रहा है

Have You Loved Enough

Have you loved enough

E n o u g h

To

Let it all fall apart
Soothe in the rains that wash the ruins away
Crumble to pieces in your head
Splash the canvas in the dead ashes
Severe to the very last bits of being
Pen life in the bloodshed

Have you loved enough
Have you loved enough to unlove

इंसान मादरचोद है

ना सफ़ेद है, ना काला
जिंदगी पेस्टल शेड्स नहीं है
अगर है तो बस धुआं धुआं

क्या सही है, क्या ग़लत है
बस एक नज़रिया है, निर्भर इस पे
देखने वालों का चश्मा साफ है या धुन्धला

इंसानियत बस एक मोहरा है
समाज बस एक ढोंग है
चेहरा नाम का नकाब पहने

इंसान आखिर मादरचोद है
I'm Scared Of Days But I'm Scared Of Nights More

I'm scared of days
But I'm scared of nights more

When the lights are dimmed out and the hustles of the citylife have retired for the day
I lie wide awake, my tightly shut eyelids trying hard to convince me to fall asleep
While the insides of my very existence lie wide awake
Staring into the abyss of the darkness of my four walls
Negotiating for regrets to be forgiven as experiences

While wondering, in the depths of it's messed up flesh

When do you run out of second chances?
When do you know you've had enough?
When do you say to yourself, "this is it"?
Do you keep piling onto the corpses of your expectations until the day you pile on as a corpse, dead from existing?
Or do you let go of it all, because you've bled a whole lot, and can't afford more dying expectations?
Where do you draw the line, which one's fair?

Once you've lived enough, you've died enough
Do you live enough till you cease to exist?

Or, do you live enough till you choose to exist?

<u>अंत से शुरू</u>

अंत से शुरू करते हैं

शुरू से शुरू का अंत तो देख लिया है हमने

शायद अंत से शुरू करने से अंत भी शुरूआत हो

www.ingramcontent.com/pod-product-compliance
Lightning Source LLC
LaVergne TN
LVHW041626070526
838199LV00052B/3261